Getting Out of My Head

… with Poems from My Heart

Confessional Poetry

by

Kristina Robertson

From my heart to yours, thank YOU.

Getting Out of My Head … with Poems from My Heart

I have never been one to share my written poetry on public forums because I have always been either insecure, or cautious towards family or the person I wrote the poem about. I have always been known for my confessional work, never shying away from the things that can make even me a bit uncomfortable. I am aware that this book is a bit of a risk and that I am taking a huge leap of faith putting it out to the public.

Writing has always been therapeutic, while performing my poetry has always felt very cathartic. But, having said all that, I can still get triggered by the person or things that once brought me pain.

Though some of these wounds have healed years ago, these poems are a reflection of me and the woman I am today.

For example, "EXstasy" is a poem that starts with just a tiny glimpse of feeling that good high while in a new relationship. But like any drug or toxic relationship, the come down became dark and ugly. That part of the poem is still very difficult for me to read out loud. It brings me back to those dreadful nights that I never in my dreams wanted to relive again. I had learned to move on. I found my voice again and though I went through many more heart breaks after, the woman I am today is strong, courageous and I wear my scars with pride. Some of these poems are merely reflections of those scars.

I survived trauma. I just hope some of these poems can at least inspire others to open up, talk about the difficult things they are afraid to say because being vulnerable is bravery. You never know who may need to hear your story.

Poetry saved me and it has often given me closure and the ability to let go.

And finally, I recognized how truly worthy I am for a love that heals, and not a love that hurts. I hope this all resonates with my words because this is my heart wrapped in a poem.

This is my confessional poetry and I sincerely thank you for reading.

Contents

In My Skin

Into Darkness

Healing

Contents

Loved

Compassion

Part One:

In My Skin

Me
Age 6

Eyes Pried Open

Crescent moon eyes
gazing into the Red Lotus Sea,
petals propagated by hints of uncertainties.

A lost American millennial,
searching inside a mother's womb for identity.
Face mixed with hesitation,
hidden beneath a father's redwood tree.

A privileged name
yet mocked and shamed,
blending fusion with confusion,
presumed adoption is to blame.

A merciless small town,
filled with slant-eyed gestures,
stereotypes and slights cut right to the core until it
festers.

I am a canvas,
painted into a camouflaged question mark,
a tsunami rippling through my ribcage.
Curves shaped into pink lotuses,
freckles connect me into an exclamation point.

My crescent moon eyes
meditate behind a reserved smile.
Bashful of my overbite,
an oversight,
but tonight,
I fight,
to just be.

Simply hers and his,
mixed,
without the division or betwixt
amidst a lunar eclipse
seen in my eyes pried wide open.

The Mask

I wear this mask for protection,
but my eyes cannot mask my disconnection.
I am here standing outside of my body,
confessing with my reflection,
that perfection is merely a rejection
of all preconceived recollections.
Perfection is unattainable.
Yet, I strive for the explainable,
of being unbreakable
to my struggle daily to be me,
to be free.

30 Minutes

If all I get to see of you,
is for 30 minutes in 365 days,
let's not look at pictures in my cell phone
to summarize what I have been up to.
Remove the superficial shield you make shifted,
the day you decided to abandon me.
Dig deep in the back of your eyes for the memory,
of Bill Withers songs and bear hugs,
for my embrace could close our next visit.
I used to respire only for you,
but my lungs will eventually swell out its last breath.
And when the 29th minute nears,
don't say the word love,
if it's a force pulling you inside solitude.
I will cup your fragile face,
thank you for giving me this life,
but promise me 31 minutes next time
so, I have something to live for.

In My Skin

When I stand before you naked,
I want you to see me beyond this flesh.
Find my neurotic bones where I have stored all my
secrets.
For every antidepressant taken has failed to suppress
my trust.
I am broken,
yet shrouded with conviction,
desperate for acceptance of my obsessive superstitions.
My vulnerability exposed.
As I start to put back on my layers,
clothed in expectation.
A hunger grows inside of me to establish my worth.
While finding comfort in my own skin,
my rebirth from within.

Ever Clear

In the sobering daylight,
I was lost and jaded,
tapping my fingers relentlessly for a quick sip of
reality.
For I am the half empty glass on the verge of spilling,
a halo hovering above a beer bottle at 2 a.m.
I can see through me,
clear as vodka,
a distilled potency,
ever clear,
ever-so-clearly,
I can see clear like purified water.
Chasing these gin-soaked memories,
as my intuition flows like waterfalls.
A toast to clarity,
seeing through my façade,
inside the hurricane glass.
My liver never loved me,
so, I learned to live without it.

I Never Knew

I am mixed Thai, Chinese, Scottish, Irish and
Cherokee.
But I feel all people see is a Twinkie.

Filing a client Chi-Man Ku's taxes,
I addressed his label last name, first:
Ku, Chi-Man.
Laughter came easy at his expense.

My father never taught me to drive.
He said Asians had bad peripherals.
The DMV failed me twice,
convinced it was my eyes and not my experience.

Once, an Asian poet called me offensive,
and I told him it was just a joke,
like the word "chink" from a boy I had a crush on in
high school,
or the way my classmates pulled at the sides of their
eyes.

My father once referred to Asians as Chinamen.
He is not Asian.
I am not adopted.
I resemble the "chinky-eyed masochist" who left him.

My mother sinned all over Bangkok.
Brought to this country to babysit her new father's
children,
I was a mistake made while using my father to escape.
She never loved him, but credits him with her new life
outside of her family.

My father loves me, but when he looks at me, I know
he sees her.

The girl who used him and disappeared with his
kindergartner.
He fought for me, and when I was ten, I chose with the
mediator to leave her.
She tells me to this day, she "let me" go.

I was born into America, no cultural residue.
From a generation of interracial unions and mixed
babies.
I have a mouth that will cut like a katana.
I was not taught to be weak and submissive.

I am neither exotic nor eager to please like a geisha.
Refusing to sit still and look pretty,
I find myself sitting still and trying to look pretty,
and for that, I am a contradiction.

"Reading Rainbow" taught me I could be
anything I wanted to be when I grew up.
It taught me which box I could check,
to allow me to be white collar instead of red dress.

As a child, I learned to loathe this dark hair, this skin.
Through my slanted eyes I only saw my father's view.
His ignorance and anger at my mother assaulting me
instead of her.
I have created an image onstage for people who look
nothing like me.

I was often the token "me love you long time" girl.
I made jokes, and the jokes were just merely hypocrisy.

I refused to get revolutionary,
yet hold my fist high for Asian Pride.

I tattoo the word "Poetry" on my back in Thai,

but don't recognize the script.
I have worn a t-shirt emblazoned "Everyone Loves an
Asian Girl,"
but never loved that description of me.

I am sorry.

I have always stood under the sunlight for my freckles
to radiate.
I have never let the Pacific Islands touch my toes.
I have never had the patience to learn about Thailand.
It is a piece of me, no matter how much I joke.

I never knew how sharp the words were that dug
through my skin.
I never knew how the effect I could have on people that
look like me.
I never knew how disrespectful I was to my mother and
my lineage,
or how Asian Americans could see me
as a racist.

Misunderstood

I want to be understood,
yet I forget to understand,
that when I get out of hand
and demand too much of myself,
I become weak.
So, I seek for your critique
and encourage us to speak our truth,
even if muttered behind clenched teeth.
Let us embrace tonight,
binds like ivy twisting tight,
while it radiates all the light within us,
despite how contrite we might feel,
on this lonely night we reveal.
When we are skin to skin,
we have always been just inches
from the beginning of understanding,
if in fact we were only ever to be misunderstood.

Part Two:

Into Darkness

EXstasy

My lover is flirtatiously high,
and I am a junkie for his smack.
We drug ourselves to enhance our desires,
and I desire him like centrifugal force.
Rolling to trip-hop,
our eyes buck and sway for each other.
We are lucky in love after three pills a night.
How appropriate that this drug,
comes stamped with clover leaves and horseshoes.
The chemical connection between us
brands our love with its name:

Ecstasy,
Clarity,
Essence,
Decadence,
Sweeties,
Speed for lovers.

And my heart beats fast, intense for him,
vibrates like the dance floor,
when his breath traces my silhouette,
licks every goose bump like chocolate chips on my
skin.
We rise like the bright white moon,
but when we come down,
everything turns black and blue as the shadow of
sobriety.

My lover is nothing but my drug dealer.
Swallows candy pills
at raves, house parties, poetry slams.
Spanks random girls over barstools,
flirts with his clients for free I-phones,

and comes down to call me crazy.

"It's just business, baby,
I come home to you, baby,
I choose to be with you…
baby."

And when he punctuates the sentiment
by taking his love to my face,
all he can say it that it wasn't a fist,
it was an open hand.
And it wasn't five pummels to the face
but 4, 3, 2,
one friend told me he said I was crazy,
and that I beat my own jaw black and blue.

Calls my bruises beauty marks.
My lover covers me with broken blood vessels.
My heart beats for more beats in fast forward.
Makes me beg on my knees until I become the little
bitch, he says I am.

"I am sorry for hitting you Bitch,
but you are crazy."

When we get high, we are lucky in love,
but the comedown turns my beauty marks to track
marks.
This euphoric high is not the answer to his problems.
And he is not the answer to mine.
And this drug cannot be used for couples counseling.

No longer his concubine or his punching bag,
if I am crazy,
it's only for ever calling this chemical connection
love.

Disconnect

We haven't spoken in months,
yet we sit across from each other this very moment.
We are concealed behind our cell phones.
Daydreaming our escape,
where technology does not exist,
and hand-held devices burn within the palm of our hands.
We only hope and pray, then, that we can find the words to speak,
what we wouldn't dare say online,
and rekindle the flame of our desires,
one less swipe at a time.

What if it Was All Me?

I was like a lemon slice in boiling water,
leaching just enough bitterness,
to my own doing.
I was a narcissistic violinist,
self-involved to my acrimonious symphony.
One-night stands refused take me seriously.
Triggered by my consequences,
thinking I could change each apathetic person into
choosing me.
Insecurity is the imbalance I walked with,
No change,
no growth.
If it meant mending my broken heart with an adhesive
bandage.
Wounds can only heal with truth,
accepting that rejection is like a promise
and change comes when I bleed,
abandoning my own deceit.
I became enough,
when I learned to drink the lemon straight,
my accountability became our fate.

Addicted to My Pain

He said he didn't want to keep breaking me,
saw the pleading look in my sweltering eyes.
Hopeless, exposed, and jaded from nothing but past
lies.
I had concealed my dimness for him like an
encumberment prize,
when its affection and connection I emphasized to yet
another wrong guy.

But what if I just wanted him to break me?
Shatter me into a million more pieces,
I have been broken before for more soul wrenching
reasons.
I begged him to just penetrate me deeply with all of his
fake sweetness,
if it meant letting my self-worth reach its culmination
while my body releases.

He said, what if indeed this is true,
all the sweetness and promises were nothing but tools.
But what if he knew right from the very start,
and he still put me together just to break me back apart.

I craved his consistency to further reject me.
As I pushed and pulled at his unwilling hesitancy to
fracture me incessantly.

I became addicted to the exquisite pain of wanting
someone so unattainable.
What is love, but lust without my darkest shame?
I give and beg too much to the undeserved while I end
up making myself look insane.

What is fragmented without my bareness to heal?
Let go, drain out the sorrow inside so I can finally feel.

When it's more than a desire for physical touch that I
appeal,
but to know I am more than enough while trying to
break my own chaotic wheel.

I dissolved into his shuddering embrace that night,
as I clutched him tightly from fear of losing him,
unwilling to put up another fight.
He wiped my tears, caressed my face with soft kisses
under the window shades of moonlight.

He told me, what if we could rewrite our past and we
never got hurt,
because I never settled for guys who didn't value my
worth.
And then he found me whole and held me and told me,
you're mine,
what if we could turn back time?

I woke up to another empty bed.
I am nothing more but a masochist who understands
the hostage I kept instead.
We are all worthy of an emotionally safe, predictable,
loving relationship he said,
but it was my destructive path that became like a
festering disease that spread.

I can only then comprehend what it's like to make
amends,
in order to fully transcend into a mended version of the
victim I would often pretend.
Love even my broken-hearted self and find being alone
through my strength all over again.
He said he didn't want to keep breaking me,
only I could ever fall in love to my unreciprocated
pain.

Winter is Coming

I am trapped inside this chaotic whiteout of a snow
globe,
tilted until all the snowflakes evaporate into thin air.
Bear this snowstorm trapped inside my perpetual
severity of a forecast.
Press me into the glass.
Shield my beating frostbitten heart inside my chest.
Touch me with slightest warmth of your callused
hands.
Together, we can create an inferno within this force
field.
Force feed me your uncertainties,
melt away all of my insecurities.
Help me shatter the glass.
So, when I finally make it out unscathed,
take my hand as we walk two steps forward,
but don't ever let your wind push me back.

Exit Music (for a Poem)

There was nothing poetic about us.
We were literal, matter-of-fact turned pessimistic.
I was a hollowed shell,
several organs with no blood running inside.
You wanted to connect with anything,
something,
someone else.
When you left,
silence descended upon me.
My heart stopped,
only to be resuscitated nonsensically.
I feared my execution,
only to regain perception.
I became the inevitable phenomenon,
high peaks and valleys in the EKG,
brought my broken heart to its resurrection.
I became optimistic.
You were merely the blood clot in my regression.
I hold onto this vessel tightly with protection,
surrender to this new verse,
while finding beauty and safe love after trauma
becomes my ultimate poetic justice.

Letting Go of Your Static

My ex would sleep with the fan on.
He was comforted in his own reverie,
a soothing white noise,
enclosed by masses of THC and treachery.
I woke up every morning sick,
unbeknownst to me,
that relationship was detrimental to my health.
When he left,
it was still heart-rending,
for I didn't know who I was without all the static.
Unalterable,
unchanging,
distortion.
Even the TV's ambient light signaled me into more
agitation.
I still felt trapped,
even when alone.
I walked in a dark cloud for months,
no desire to grow.
The first step is to acknowledge and accept your own
burden.
Letting go is so much easier to say than do.
But when its hissing sound finally stops,
I exhaled all the trauma.
I can think clearly,
sleep soundly,
consistently,
alone,
and most importantly,
next to the one who was meant for me.

Yours and Mine, Intertwined - 2024
2nd Story at Red Rock Coffee, Mountain View
Photo: by Anthony Lê

Part Three:

Healing

Reflection

In times of sorrow,
seek for positivity.
Your reflection guides.

The Hummingbird

I've lost track of the days secluded inside,
the deep breaths of relief I've taken in stride.
All the calories consumed and number of pounds,
yet, in my room, I stay in tuned by the hummingbird
sounds;
shrill wing whistles as they beat their wings.
A vibration that hovers and harmoniously sings.
It's the song I long to hear every dreadful day,
I hope and I pray that it won't fly away.

Fireflies

I lost my radiance during a heavy storm,
faded into darkness,
overcast with zero breaks in between.
I begin looking for my missing glow.
I searched for fireflies,
sat near dying bonfires,
as they blinked on and off in the distance.
Most female fireflies can't fly,
they can only dream about soaring without wings.
I chased them instead,
with hopes of catching my own brilliance blowing in
the ocean breeze.
When I caught one,
he was a good omen,
inspiration and fortune,
whose wings were never broken, nor spoken.
If there was any conviction left in me,
I would have to reciprocate his flashes with my own
light.
True love can endure the darkest of clouds.
But I wasn't lost,
I was found.
For there was a radiance that always lived deep inside
of me.
I just needed to be seen in the dark.
I just needed to survive the storm.

To the One Who Helped Me Heal

You met me when I was completely broken,
from a love that was so toxic that became so triggering
and unspoken.
I leaned on you a lot on those dark and lonely nights.
Patiently listened to me without judgement, always
making sure I was alright.
You were the one who walked into my life when it felt
the rest of the world walked out.
You believed in my worth, protecting me while putting
an end to all of my self-doubt.
True selfless friendships are admittedly rare,
who want nothing but the best for you without motives,
a kind soul who genuinely cares.
Thank you for finding me lost in my darkest place,
cradled my fragile heart in your warm embrace and
shielded me into such a safe space.
You led me back into the light,
where I have healed from those who couldn't
understand me.
And in this last year, you were the best gift I needed to
see,
gratefully there you were, my sweet bestie,
with open arms and filled with such sweet empathy.

A Woman Rising

She kneeled into his submission.
She was always his vision,
a portrait of his control to dominate her every decision.
She became jaded,
resistant,
here lies her naked truth;
from constant scorn to emotional abuse.
She can't recognize herself beyond her flesh,
exposed yet shrouded with conviction.
She was clothed in the expectation
to always give in and say yes,
but it is her scars that shade different.
She waters her soul,
plant seeds in her mind,
opens herself as a lotus flower would.
She is resilient to the sun,
susceptible under the moon.
She learned,
kneeling is her prayer that seeks worship.
Her worn body curved into her own sculpture.
Arms painted around her bends,
arched back,
bruised knees,
craned neck to better view her own light.
She is of love and light,
but wears her darkness like armor.
She has been dishonored in her own skin,
a rebirth within.
This woman,
handles her tired work with the softness of her
silhouette,
and the trigger in her eyes.
She started to tell him no,
but yes, to herself.
She kneels for rest,

her blemishes confess at every sunrise,
for every sacrifice, she realizes
she is worth so much more than what he has ever
denied.
She may be a woman kneeling,
but never forget how far she has come,
for she is also a woman rising.

Love Me or Hate Me

Pull my stems and roots,
yet I still thrive in the soil,
propagating strong.

Seasons

I would wither in the summer,
sprouting grief into dry soil.
He was just another seed from a dandelion,
dispersal of my wishes through the autumn breeze.
I was just tedious,
impassively plucked petals,
pricked thistles from my heart.
I became indifferent,
a vase half empty
while he poured more into my cup.
Patiently tending to my garden,
flourishing from tranquility.
I started to turn over a new leaf.
Progressed,
grounded,
into a pragmatist in love.
While thriving deep inside of me,
I began to blossom in spring.

Mother Earth

I slowly drift out into the Red Lotus Sea,
petals propagated by reflective uncertainties.
Stirring my limbs feverishly,
I feel as if I am drowning.
A hallowed seashell,
silenced from the rolling waves.
Find me running barefoot in the forest,
grounded to the dirt,
hair blowing crossly in the wind.
I stumble on the branches and fall into Mother Earth.
Her vibration shudders the tips of my fingers,
I lay like I was 2:50 on a clock,
stretching every muscle while emerging from nature's
womb.
This American soil is my sanctuary.
I am like a dandelion blowing in a hurricane,
wishing to feel poised in my own mixed freckled skin.
I smell the moss and wet tree trunks,
purest air to breathe.
I breathe it all in and out,
And fall back into the sea of empathy haloing my body,
riding the waves of my emotions.
I tread softly,
reflect underneath the surface of my confusion.
Floating to allow the salt to heal my apprehension.
Remembering that I am never alone on this Earth
when I have my mother and her roots inside.

In Your Sea of Love

I walked on fire
until I reached your ocean.
Burned coals,
stranded me to uncertainty,
flame-spouting from all those love bombs
until I became extinguished.
Filled my aching lesions with salt.
You, persistent like a hurricane,
I was set blazing.
When you finally saved me,
hydrated me back to life.
Most scabs will fall away,
but the scars remain,
or wounds that heal.
I know loving me is like watering an inferno,
but your tenderness flows incessantly and silently.
Water does not resist,
water is patient.
And when the smoke finally cleared,
I began to flourish in your sea.

Under One Moon

I swim against the deep-water current,
he waits for me beneath the ocean floor.
Drifting further into abyss,
unsettled by the vibration
created from my atmospheric turbulence.
Grasping for a breath,
I finally touched the surface.
The salt water becomes vulnerary.
He wraps me like a life jacket,
as I clutch him tightly
longing signs of light.
His purity rectifies my hesitation,
reminding me that
drowning is never an option.
We are bound by this hallowed sea,
when the crest becomes too steep,
I rise from my own vulnerability.
I dreamt of him,
through its canal's reflection.
But it was always just me,
I would see,
my flesh in constant distress,
days became weeks,
weeks become months,
and the nights never seemed to end.
The darkness casts no shadow,
and somehow,
it was he that became my light illuminating around the bend.
Eclipsed by an uncertain tomorrow,
his love treads water so naturally,
I bid good night to this lonely sorrow,
under one moon,
we reflect over the marine,
rescued by his radiance,
a halo unveils his love for me even on my darkest night.

Photographer: Amy King
www.amyelizabethportraits.com

Part Four:

Loved

Connecting With Someone So Deep

Connecting with someone so deep.
Reprieved, sheltered from the storm.
Temptation led to propinquity,
embracing the tiniest of flaws.

Reprieved, sheltered from the storm.
Consistency is just the foreplay.
Embracing the tiniest of flaws,
and we climax without touch.

Consistency is just the foreplay.
Temptation led to propinquity,
and we climax without touch.
Connecting with someone so deep.

Chromatics

He loved the way the sunlight glistened off me.
Engulfed by my radiance,
mesmerized by my prismatic pallet of colors.
I was a ray of light,
inviting inspiration and poetry.
He basked in my illumination,
my sparkle of joy,
a beacon of hope to his darkened sorrow.
I was his mosaic of light,
I was his muse,
he couldn't erase or refuse.
I was a poem he had written
in the middle of a long lonely night.
Lusting for the sunrise,
dreaming I would come into the light.
I would come in his life.

I Am Easy to Love After All

I overlook his splendor wrapped around the vines,
between the tendrils and thorns
for a tenderness I never knew.
He begs me in my dreams,
gazes into me at sunset,
waters me at sunrise,
I become the fallen leaf
receding into the soil.
It's that echo in the canyon that reminds me I am hard to
handle.
I am the caterpillar refusing to spin itself into a silky cocoon.
I design butterflies from the dirt like dusty snow angels,
my makeshift wings form and flutter away into dust.
I am the tornado blowing into his concrete love.
He chooses me today,
and every day.
When the wind touches my face,
it's the soft fragments of his kisses,
a reassurance that I am seen even through my resistance.
As someone who is easy to love,
through his unwavering persistence.

He Loves Me!

I plucked the last petal,
exposing only the peduncle.
My love had finally budded.
No longer the puff pulled out and shunned from sunlight,
dispersing my apprehension through the stiff breeze,
he found me beautiful even in the fertile soil,
blooming early and virtually last.
We became magic when the fluff was blown,
making this the ultimate season of consistency,
my wish had finally come true.

Free As a Butterfly

My heart was overwhelmed,
deep inside the cocoon.
In its hidden glory of benevolence,
while sleeping in hibernation.
My love,
like a caterpillar,
all that heaviness,
learned patience,
stirring restlessly,
evolving while curing,
until my wings formed and fluttered.
I flew by him countless times,
But somehow missed.
Consciously, until I knew.
I use to play with way too many spiders,
who only preyed on butterflies,
until I soared to his hyacinth.
Where I could be unapologetically me,
who loves freely
and finally loved in return.

What Happens When a Poet Meets Her Muse

I clutch onto his every word,
cling to the beating pulse of his heart like syllables to a
haiku.
Trace the outline of his smile,
his ball point pen to my open journal.
A page that smells of old love letters to Robert Browning,
he is my first edition,
warm, deep and subtly seductive,
an endless poem that feels so intimate and inviting.
I come all over,
I write into him,
line after line,
sheets covered in ink stains shaped like an exclamation
point.
This is what it feels to be so inspired,
when chaos discovers euphoria,
when a poet meets her muse.

Captivated

Sometimes I open my eyes just a crack
to watch you sleep.
Place my hand gently on your heart,
counting the number of times your chest rises,
baptized by your fastened eyes.
When I finally match your breath,
I fall back to earth,
knowingly,
it wasn't a dream,
I was tranced by this reality.

A Sunday Kind of Love

We walked across the same pier,
exactly one year ago today.
Like magic, the rain cleared,
sun bursting with sincerity.
We smell of salt water and churros,
simplicity adorned with our hungry eyes.
Sea breeze collided into us,
holding hands, tenderly.
I knew I wanted him then,
licking our lips, lustfully.
Brushing windblown hair with willing fingers,
I lingered by the brisk shore.
But surely, it was his warmth I felt,
its serenity poured all over me.
It was then I knew,
chivalrously, walking street side of me,
listening intently,
consistently,
while sea lions bark incessantly,
and lounge underneath the rays,
on a Sunday kind of love.

Collaboration

The fluorescent strobe lights are bouncing off my retinas,
like the mattress we used to shake the earth with.

There, my muse,
fingers guitar strumming the work of my own hands,
into long burning, unrequited song notes.

My eyes shutter and dance,
lips curve,
hips buck and sway to the sound beat of his acoustic ballad.

Synthesizing me with such sweet simplicity,
I feel it from my lower back to my thighs.
The sound he plays resembles
the faint grunts he makes when inspiring deeper.

I wonder,
how much he knows
what his haunting voice does to me.
As I cross my legs tighter,
fingers gripping into the couch cushions,
while he amplifies my hunger for his -

slapping of the bass lines,
pounding on the jembe,
blowing tantalizing whispers through the flute.

I know what good music is.
It's in his love wrapped in rhythms of the banjo,
it's recorded through the soundboard,
inside the depth of my walls.

I know later tonight,
we will collaborate.

The drum bass will echo off the walls like our upstairs
neighbors
knocking to the sound of our collaboration
against the love seat,
the coffee table,
the sliding glass door.

This stage is only ours.
I love when we make music together.

Coffee Lover

Eyes half open,
with the thought of your taste,
has me grinding.
Anticipating,
the release of your aroma upon my senses.
It's steaming inside,
whistling like a kettle on a stove,
filling my cup to its brim.
The rich nutty taste upon my lips,
cream coats my tongue.
Nirvana penetrates my body,
stimulating the mind.
My eyes wide open,
primed to seize the day.

Protected

Inserted in it's eager to open wrapper.
Easily to place
in my pocket, wallet,
or on a silver platter.
Surrounds the
freshly lit candles,
rumpled sheets,
rose pedals on the floor,
"Let's Get It On" by Marvin Gaye,
a half open bottle of Dom Perignon.
Two sweaty bodies collide.
once placed,
rubbery, rough with a lubricated cave-like delicatessen
inside,
a circular orb almost ring worm like shaped
stretches to six, maybe seven, maybe eight inches of
pleasurable delight.
Heavenly rainbow starbursts taste of tropical heaven in my
mouth.
Or my personal favorite car freshener scent: Strawberry.
A flavor for each dazzling color.
Red like the freshly applied Revlon lipstick on my already
puckered cherry lips.
Blue is your handsome radiant eyes which penetrate right
through mine.
Green reminds me of your 1999 Toyota Corolla with
"hydraulics."
Protected we are all night,
Shh, let's not talk anymore.
Just finish the champagne.

Yours and Mine, Intertwined – 2024
Hotel Utah, San Francisco
Photo by J. Valencia Photography

Part Four:

Compassion

Empathy

When your partner's down,
be their safe space to turn to.
Be soft when it's hard.

80/20

I held his head in disbelief,
after I scolded him for hours.
He told me he felt so alone,
unbeknownst, I was sustaining my power.

Nobody is perfect, they would say,
and perfect is most definitely not me.
He has only held me in such a high regard,
so why couldn't I show mercy or love him unconditionally?

This wasn't even directed at me,
he just needed me to be a safe space.
And now he is afraid to be vulnerable,
I couldn't handle his own failure with grace.

To practice empathy, I must imagine myself in his place,
make him feel seen and heard,
because some days he may need a little more from me,
a shoulder to lean on, as his someone most preferred.

Sometimes we can't be everything, *(we can most certainly try)*
I recognize his pain and value his worth.
He doesn't ever have to feel alone,
I am here for him while continuing to do my part of the work.

A Retractable Love

Sometimes,
you and I struggle,
like we are tangled in a slinky.
My mood swings like a metal spring that stretches,
wrapped around our waists,
pull you in,
push me out.
Our hearts are the sound of expanding and collapsing.
I am the two seconds before the first domino fell.
My love,
is a chain reaction in linear sequence.
You become intractable,
stagnant to my Murphy's Law.
We are a sling shot away from falling down another flight of
stairs,
but anything that can go wrong,
somehow turns perfectly right,
when we become retractable from acceptance.

A Poem for My Future Mother-in-Law

Will you dance with him under the stars of his father?
Hug and sway to "Bridge over Troubled Water."
How you held his head high with two grieving eyes,
raised him up,
watched him fail,
but never doubted he would thrive.
Could we ever fill a heavy void left in such a traumatic loss?
While he was still learning to be the man you all aspired him
to be.
You carried him in your womb,
you carried the courage for both,
and what a wonderful man he turned out to be.
What a wonderful man he is to me.
I know your love for him is endless,
I can only hope to match your devotion,
trusting me with this piece of your heart that is your son.

Facing My Fears

At the start of my sound journey,
we lay next to each other with our arms touching.
There were drums, and then a flute that echoed a witch's
cackle.
It was uncanny,
a place I didn't want to go but it was pulling me there.
As I drifted more into obscurity,
I became instantly unsettled to the vibration of the beat.
It felt like I was pushing my way through everything and
anything to get to him,
finding his sanctuary.
I was scared to be in the darkness, walking down a staircase
leading to nowhere.
I could still feel his breath; it gave me a sense of hope.
I wiggled my toes on the concrete to reaffirm that I am still
here.
I exist with this thrashing heart.
I kept telling myself to be fearless on this passage.
The hairs on my neck stood up and swayed to the heavy
pulsate of my core.
I wanted to hold him, but I am too drained.
I cannot carry my love and walk down these stairs in the
dark.
It's just too much.
My body feels so heavy.
My heart feels like its pounding to break free.
My ribcage is a caterpillar's prison cell and it's gnawing its
way out.
I desperately hung onto the static of his arm hairs,
gasping for a breath.
He promised he would never leave me in a panicked state,
Yet, when you constantly have anxiety like I do, it feels like
you are confined in your cocoon.
The drums stop,
The echoes dissipate,

The clouds' part and it rained every tear drop I dreaded to illustrate.
I exhaled,
followed my heart beat to the santoor,
tuning each unit of strings to a frequency beside me.
I could feel its luminosity burning in the back of my throat,
surrounded by thousands of tiny embers,
igniting my apprehension.
I looked at my reflection in the water and saw the beauty I always wish I had.
Hidden behind my insecurities,
facing vulnerability.
As I slowly felt myself detaching from him,
I began to peel layers of my casing.
It felt like he had freed the butterfly from my ribcage,
I flap my wings and surrender to the melody.
When the music stopped, I opened my eyes;
To find him beside me, relentlessly haloing my trepidation.
There will always be things I am going to be frightened to do alone,
but allowing it to consume me will keep me sheathed in my asylum.
But with each unwearied breath,
it will eventually guide me to my wings so I can fly away from it all,
and that is what I am most anxious for.

A Forgotten Pregnancy

I clutch my empty stomach
like a featherless pillow.
It's light and airy,
insubstantial,
tender to the touch.
The emptiness churns for empathy.
I feel like a hollowed-out tree stump,
depleted even in the soil.
I eat to feel brimmed with worth,
overload myself with vibrancy.
Expectancy,
to feel anything but nothing.
I dream my womb is a cocoon,
filled with butterflies fluttering incessantly.
As caterpillars climb the pillars of my ovaries,
daydreaming of a forgotten pregnancy.

Back to the Beginning

When we are born,
we open our eyes, hopefully, for the first time to
unconditional love.
We are exquisiteness swaddled in our own world of
perfection.
We become the creators to excellence,
survival wishes are at the edge of our fingertips.
As we experience pain for the first time,
emotional, gut-wrenching, earth-shattering heartache,
when we are taught judgment and intolerance,
when we are born equal shaping into a division sign,
when we are made to feel less than ideal,
and it feels as if the womb swallows us back into the
darkness.
We quickly rush to sleep so we can dream.
We guard our wishing well tightly to our chest so no one will
steal our identity.
We become faceless to our own light.
We are the humming bird lodged in our throat,
singing our way out.
We must learn to communicate with our heart beats.
We must discover how to break the glass,
show off our blemishes like they were our triumphs.
Be still,
Be silent,
close our eyes while we blow on the dandelion seeds to wish
us all back to the beginning,
When we were all unknown,
opening our eyes for the first time to unconditional love.

Acknowledgements

"Eyes Pried Open"
Appeared in "The Mixed Issue" – Overachiever Magazine, 2020

"I Never Knew"
Appeared in Experimental & Form Poetry / Better than Starbucks, 2020

"Mother Earth"
Published in "Asian American Healing: A Nature Walk Guide" by Chopsticks Alley Art, 2024

Front Cover Art by Catrina Sida. Thank you, my friend for allowing me to use "Hope" as my cover. I was deeply connected to this piece. In 2021, I felt so lost and your art and friendship most certainly gave me strength and hope.

Thank you, Esther and Paloma. It was our show "Yours and Mine, Intertwined" that brought me back to spoken word and inspired me to publish this book. You two were the soundtrack to my life and I thank you both for believing in me and my poetry.

Thank you to Sam who contributed some of the dialogue to *"Addicted to the Pain."*

"A Woman Rising" was inspired by the late Nathan Oliviera's art work: "A Woman Kneeling" – it was her eyes that spoke to me. She was me and I am a woman rising each day.

To my mom and dad. Although it wasn't easy on all of us, I know you both loved me very much and made lots of sacrifices. And I love you both so much. The poems about us were not the easiest for me to write and sharing it to this day is still difficult.

Lots of love and gratitude to Chopsticks Alley Art. Trami Cron, thank you for always believing in my poetry and celebrating my work by giving me such safe spaces to share my stories. I feel honored to be a part of your amazing team while paying it forward and helping other artists with their creative dreams.

Thank you, Brandon, for your unconditional love and support. You are my muse and inspiration for the poems in my "Loved" chapter of this book. I feel safe, seen, heard and loved by you. And I love you so much.

About the Poet

Kristina Robertson is a confessional spoken word performer and writer in Santa Clara, California. She has competed in two national poetry slam competitions. Her work has appeared in *Overachiever Magazine* and was published in Chopsticks Alley Art's *Asian American Healing: A Nature Walk Guide*. Through her work with Chopsticks Alley Art, she helps to provide platforms for fellow AAPI artists to showcase their talent all while sharing her love for poetry with her community. When she is not writing or working, she enjoys kickboxing, running, and spending time with friends, family and her partner.

You can find her on Instagram: @kristina_robertson18